Canaries

G.T. Dodwell

John Bartholomew & Son Limited
Edinburgh and London

Contents

First published in Great Britain 1976 *by*
JOHN BARTHOLOMEW & SON LIMITED
12 Duncan Street, Edinburgh EH9 1TA
And at 216 High Street, Bromley BR1 1PW

ISBN 0 7028 1071 1

1st edition

Reprinted 1978

Designed and illustrated by Allard Design Group Limited
Printed in Great Britain

History

Canaries were first introduced into Europe by the Spaniards during the sixteenth century after the conquest of the Canary Islands. In scientific literature the species was first mentioned by Conrad Gesner in his great work *Historia Animalium*, published in Zurich during the years 1551–58.

Today the canary is classified by ornithologists as a distinct race of the serin and they have given it the sub-specific title of *Serinus canarius canarius*. In addition to the islands from which it derives its name, it is also found in the wild in Madeira and in the Azores, where it is said to be a pest: a bounty was at one time paid for its destruction. It is doubtful whether many wild canaries are now exported, except perhaps as zoological specimens, because many years of domestication have brought the bird a very long way from the original, both in beauty of form and of song.

It has been suggested by some authors that for many years the Spaniards only exported male birds, either to protect their lucrative trade by preventing them from being bred in captivity or, and more likely, because only the male birds were in demand: only they, and not the females, are songsters. Since the sexes do not differ widely in appearance it is more than probable that females sometimes found their way into consignments of male birds, but whether at this stage in the history of the species anyone tried breeding the birds in captivity is doubtful.

One incident of some historical interest, so often quoted by writers that it has become part of the folklore of canaries, tells how a ship carrying a consignment of birds was wrecked off the coast of Elba. The birds escaped and soon settled on the island and established a thriving colony which lasted for a number of years; but whether this had any bearing upon the domestication of canaries in Europe is not known.

It is a fact, however, that the first published reference to their being bred in captivity came from Italy; in 1622 the writer Olina said that not only were they being successfully bred, but that there was even a surplus of birds that were being sent to Germany, Switzerland, and the Tyrol. Further confirmation of their domestication came in 1675 from the English writer Josiah Blagrove; after saying that they bred canaries 'very plentifully' in Germany and Italy, he added: 'they have bred some few here in England, though as yet not anything to the purpose that they do in other countries'. Evidently the birds at this stage had shown no divergence from

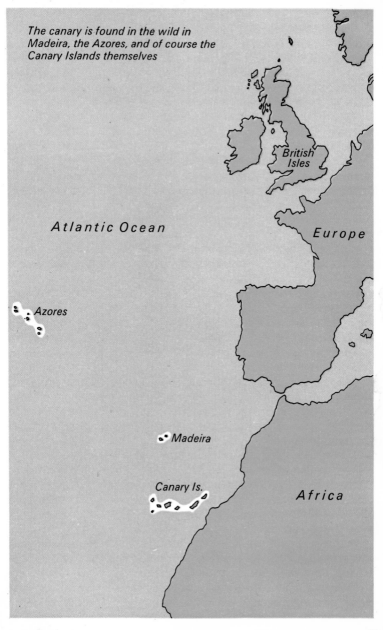

The canary is found in the wild in Madeira, the Azores, and of course the Canary Islands themselves

Atlantic Ocean

British Isles

Europe

Azores

Madeira

Canary Is.

Africa

the wild form, for Blagrove stated that most people could not distinguish a canary 'from one of our common green birds' (green-finches).

On the Continent variations in plumage as a result of the effects of domestication must have occurred in the following century, for, soon after the beginning of the eighteenth century, an important work on canaries was published in France: *Traité des Serins de Canarie* (*Treatise on Canaries*), by Hervieux. He described all of the varieties then known to him, which, in the 1713 edition of his book, amounted to no less than twenty-nine. Most of these 'varieties' are not distinct breeds as we know them today but merely common plumage variants of the canary; they are still in existence and are known to fanciers as self, foul, and variegated, both in green and cinnamon colouring.

By the middle of the eighteenth century developments were already taking place which were to lay the foundations of some of the breeds of the present day, although the ultimate perfection of many of them was probably not achieved until the Victorian era. It is to the eighteenth-century artisans of Britain and the Continent that the art of 'fancying' owes its origins. The careful breeding and selection of fancy points which appealed to them led to the emergence of clearly identifiable local types which ultimately became a major breed, or else merged with others as time went by and tastes changed.

Although the hobby was widely practised in many parts of Europe, certain places became noted as centres of canary culture; these were London and Norwich in Britain, and Antwerp, Paris, Milan, and St Andreasburg on the Continent. In London by the end of the eighteenth century there were several fanciers' societies devoted to the raising and exhibiting of canaries: at this time they were the beautiful, but now extinct, London Fancy variety. A detailed article on the subject of canary fancying in the metropolis appeared in the *Illustrated London News* of 12 December 1846, giving an account of the activities of the four societies then operating in London, together with some engravings of winning exhibition birds of the period.

To many people the name of Norwich is almost synonymous with that of canary, for that East Anglian city became one of the greatest centres of the hobby in Europe and gave its name to one of the most famous breeds of canary. By the middle of the nineteenth century the numbers of canaries which were being raised in, and around, Norwich virtually amounted to a cottage industry,

British
Isles **Norwich**

London
St. Andreasburg

Antwerp

Paris

Europe

Milan

Mediterranean

Africa

Although canaries became generally popular in eighteenth-century Europe, the towns shown made a particularly important contribution to canary culture

9

and many thousands of birds were sent up to London each year, destined for the various pet-bird markets of that city.

There is a generally accepted tradition that it was the Flemish weavers who had settled in Norfolk who were responsible for the introduction of the pastime of canary breeding into East Anglia. It is certainly true that the Flemish were very skilful fanciers and in their own homeland produced many important breeds of livestock, among them a distinctive type of canary that was to provide the foundation stock for all of the 'frilled' and 'posture' breeds of today, and quite early in the nineteenth century there were societies of fanciers in Antwerp and Ghent comparable with those of London.

A very different kind of development claimed the attention of fanciers in Germany, where, in the Hartz Mountains, canaries were prized almost entirely for their song. Here it was soon discovered that they were capable of imitating the utterances of other birds and eventually they were trained to sing to order with the aid of musical instruments. Careful breeding selection of the most accomplished performers, coupled with the patient training of each succeeding generation of young birds, has now produced a race of singing canaries whose notes are completely different from those of their wild ancestors.

During the later years of the nineteenth century canary breeding developed into a major small-livestock hobby, and many general fanciers' associations sprang up to cater for this interest. Eventually there was sufficient following for each to form its own separate society and many of the cage-bird clubs which are in existence today owe their origins to this period. The present century, with its increasing material prosperity, has seen the continued development of canary keeping as a hobby, and the fanciers of today, no less than their predecessors, are making a contribution to the history of the canary as a domestic bird. The ideas of breeders never remain entirely static and recent trends have sometimes resulted in amendments to old-established standards of perfection. There has also been the creation of entirely new varieties of considerable merit, particularly in the field of colour breeding. The standard breeds continue to receive solid support which will ensure their continuance for many years, but regrettably some of the old-fashioned varieties have suffered a period of neglect which, in some cases, has threatened their very existence. But it is pleasing to record that a revival of interest in these old breeds has recently taken place, and many fanciers are determined to preserve for posterity some of the canary heritage.

Breeds

The chief attributes of the canary which have attracted the attention of fanciers can be summarized under the headings of type (i.e. shape or form), colour, and song, and it will be a matter of convenience to deal with the various breeds in this order.

English Type Breeds. English fanciers have particularly excelled in this department to the exclusion, to some extent, of breeding for colour or song and, as a result, British breeds of canary are well known throughout the world.

Foremost among these breeds is the Border Fancy which owes its existence to fanciers on either side of the English/Scottish border who developed and perfected their birds as an exhibition-form from the ordinary common canary. As breeds go, it is not a particularly old one, the first specialist society having been formed in 1890, but it rapidly gained in popularity until today it is the most widely kept variety in the British Isles.

The Border has no really outstanding characteristic, unless it be its gay, jaunty, and lively manner, for it has been developed with the idea of achieving perfect symmetry, with no one feature predominating, so that a harmonious balance of outline is produced. It is a medium-sized bird, not exceeding $5\frac{1}{2}$ in. in length, and has a small, round, neat-looking head with the eye centrally placed and a fine, short beak. The back is well filled and nicely rounded, with a gentle rise over the shoulder, and then a straight line to the point of the tail. The breast is also well rounded, but not too prominent, and it gradually tapers towards the vent. The wings are compact and carried close to the body, just meeting at the tips a little lower than the root of the tail. The feathers of the tail, too, are closely folded and perfectly balance the body, being carried neither too high nor too low. The legs are of medium length, showing very little of the thigh, and carry the bird in a semi-erect position at an angle of about sixty degrees.

The plumage is close, firm, and fine in quality, possessing a smooth, glossy appearance without any frills or roughness. The colour should be rich, pure, and level throughout, and the practice of colour feeding (*see* chapter on Moulting) is specifically debarred. Borders are trouble-free breeders and on this account are frequently the first variety taken up by the novice.

At one time the Cinnamon canary would have been classified purely as a colour variety, but it has long since been bred for

Border Fancy

exhibition to Norwich standards so that it is, in effect, now a type breed. This variety originally stems from one of the very earliest mutations of the wild green canary and was mentioned as long ago as 1709 by the writer Hervieux. The characteristic colouring is caused by the absence of black pigmentation, leaving only brown, which, superimposed upon the yellow ground colour, produces cinnamon. In size and form this breed should be similar to a good type of Norwich canary, even a shade larger if possible. It is very important that it should have good wing carriage and a compact tail, and be of excellent feather quality, with no suggestion of 'eyebrows', which are a serious fault in Cinnamons. The colour should be of a deep, sound cinnamon throughout and not show any sign of greenish shades, nor any tendency to light feathering under the vent. This breed is generally colour-fed for exhibition: this has the effect of considerably improving the warmth and depth of tone.

It is worth noting, in passing, that canaries of cinnamon colouring are also to be found in most other breeds, and these, if kept, should of course be bred to their own particular breed standard.

There are three British breeds which sport the crested characteristic and, of these, the one in which the feature shows its most extreme development is the Crested canary. This breed was at one time known, and is still occasionally referred to, as the Crested Norwich, but it is many years now since it developed a distinct type of its own. The crest is another very early mutation which, although not mentioned by Hervieux, was added to his list by Buffon later in the eighteenth century. Basically it is a tuft of feathers sprouting from the centre of the crown of the head; in its rudimentary form it may not have been particularly attractive but, having been 'worked upon' by generations of breeders, is now quite an imposing piece of headgear.

In this breed the size and formation of the crest are almost the be-all and end-all of the bird, and many judges look no further. A crest cannot be too large and should consist of an abundance of long, broad, leafy feathers radiating in the form of a circle from a small, neat centre and drooping well over the eyes, beak, and back of the skull. Ideally this crest should appear well groomed, with no splits or breaks in its outline and no roughness in the form of 'horns' or tufty pieces of feather to spoil its symmetry.

It is a characteristic of the crested breeds of canary that there is a genetically lethal factor involved in the production of the crest

Cinnamon

Crested

which, while quite harmless in a single 'dose', renders a bird non-viable if the gene is present in a double dose. For this reason, two *crested* birds are not paired together and half of the breed consists of plain-headed birds which are mated to the crested individuals to produce 50 per cent of each type among the progeny (*see* the chapter on Breeding). In the Crested canary these plain-headed birds are called 'Crestbreds'.

Apart from the presence or absence of the actual crest, the appearance of Crest and Crestbred is identical — a massive head, a short, thick neck and a broad deep body, to some extent built on the lines of that of a bullfinch. The bird stands fairly low across the perch on shortish legs, which are well set back, and the wings and tail should be closely folded and not too long. Although Crested-canary breeders endeavour to keep the body as neat and compact as possible, good feather quality is not a notable feature of the breed since it is a near impossibility to obtain long and profuse feathering in the crest without getting it on the body as well.

In its heyday, before the First World War, spectacular prices were asked, and paid, for outstanding birds, but the breed has been steadily losing ground over the past fifty years and is now in the hands of only a few enthusiasts.

In the canary fancy, miniature forms of the various breeds have never aroused any great interest, and have generally been dismissed as mere undersized specimens of the true breed. In the Fife Fancy, however, we have a breed that has achieved acceptance even though it is, in effect, no more than a small version of Border Fancy. The breed began its separate identity in 1957, following a meeting held in Kirkcaldy; this resulted in the formation of a specialist club to preserve the breeding and exhibiting of the smaller bird at a time when there was a decided tendency towards an increase in size in normal Borders. The pictorial model and the wording of the official standard are almost identical to those of the Border Fancy, the main exception being that a total of twenty points are allotted for smallness of size; the length of the bird, it is stated, should not exceed $4\frac{1}{2}$ inches.

While the majority of our canary varieties had their origins in the nineteenth century, or earlier, the Gloster Fancy is a creation of more recent times, having made its first appearance on the show bench at the Crystal Palace in 1925. It is a breed that was 'created' by interbreeding small-sized Crested canaries, crested Roller canaries, and the smallest of Borders that were available at that time. They were skilfully blended into the small, neat, lively, and

Fife Fancy

Gloster (corona)

prolific breed which already begins to challenge the Border for first place in popularity.

As with all crested canaries there are two types which comprise the breed as a whole: the crested birds (which in the Gloster are known as 'Coronas') and the plainheads (called 'Consorts').

In the Coronas the crest should be neat, round, regular and unbroken in outline, but not so large as in the crested canary, as the eye should be clearly discernible. The consort should have a broad, well-rounded head, with a good rise over the centre of the skull and showing a heavy brow. As to bodily conformation, from the breed's inception there has always been an aim for a 'tendency to the diminutive' and show specimens should not exceed about 4¾ in. in length. Small size must not be equated with meanness, however, for the Gloster is a well-built and 'cobby' type of bird in spite of its lack of inches, and the general impression should be of a short and compact bird without any tendency towards being slim and racy.

As with other small varieties of canary, the Gloster is a very free and prolific breeder which, as in the case of the Border, often recommends it to the beginner in the canary fancy. But it should be realized that perfection on the show bench is just as difficult to achieve with these breeds as with any other.

The Lancashire is also a crested variety and has the added distinction of being the largest of all English breeds of canary, the aim of breeders being to attain 8 in. as an ideal length. The crested individuals are known as 'Coppies' and their consorts simply as 'Plainheads'. The Lancashire is always bred in the clear form (i.e. clear yellow, or clear buff — see chapter on Breeding) with no variegation in the plumage, such as is found in other breeds of canary. The coppies are, however, permitted to have a grey, or grizzled, crest without incurring disqualification on the show bench.

The Lancashire is a very old breed and is thought to have been developed from birds brought to Britain by Flemish weavers in the eighteenth century. It reached the peak of its career in late Victorian times, but strangely enough it was never very popular for its own sake, except in its native country, England. It was widely used by breeders with the object of developing or improving other varieties, notably the Crest and the Yorkshire, and demands that were made upon Lancashire stocks for this purpose started a decline in their numbers. This decline continued throughout the present century and the last pure-bred stocks of Lancashires

Lancashire – plainhead

apparently vanished during the Second World War. Present-day enthusiasts are attempting to recreate the variety from the breeds to which it contributed in the past and some very reasonable specimens have already been produced.

Although included among the 'type' canaries, the Lizard is in a class of its own, for it is the only variety now kept entirely for the marking of its plumage, unique in the canary world. It is the oldest existing breed of show canary and was clearly described as a fancier's speciality in an old manual dated 1762. The mutation which gave rise to the distinctive feather pattern is believed to have occurred in France and, traditionally, the bird owes its introduction into Britain to the Huguenot refugees.

The most important of the markings are the 'spangling' on the back and the 'rowing' on the breast, formed by a series of black, crescent-shaped spots, clearly outlined with a lacing of gold or silver. Fanciers also attach great importance to the feather quality and to the depth and richness of the ground colour of their birds; the birds are normally colour-fed to improve these points. The Lizard also has sound, glossy, dark wings and tail, with no light or grizzled feathers to spoil their beauty, and dark beak and legs, even down to black toe-nails. Perhaps the most eye-catching feature is the 'cap' which is an area of ordinary yellow feathers on the crown of the head — the only light feathers in the Lizard's make-up. Ideally it should be of a perfect oval, or thumb-nail, shape, roughly following the line of the skull and passing just above the eye from which it is separated by a thin line of dark feathers called the 'eyelash'.

Owing to the unusual nature of the mutation, the Lizard is only in perfect show plumage in its first year, after which a slight deterioration occurs with each successive moult, thus presenting the fancier with the annual challenge of breeding a fresh batch of exhibition youngsters.

Probably the best known of all canaries, at least by name, is the Norwich, which has made the name of that East Anglian city famous throughout the canary world. Well before the middle of the nineteenth century the breed had established itself as the leading exhibition variety and was to remain so for almost three quarters of a century. From the 1880s onwards changes began to take place in the breed which were brought about as a result of outcrossings in pursuit of new ideas. After an unsettled period of a few years, an important breeders' conference was held in 1890 which drew up a new standard: this has remained basically unchanged.

Lizard

Norwich

The Norwich is a largish breed of about $6\frac{1}{2}$ in. in length, but it is bulk rather than length which is its most noticeable feature, for it is a broad, cobby, thickset bird with a short, wide back, deeply curved breast, thick neck, and a bold and massive head. The wings and tail are short and well braced, and the legs are strong and well set back, giving the bird a stance at an angle of about forty-five degrees. Colour has always been an important attribute of the Norwich and should be of a deep-orange tone, brought about, once again, as a result of colour feeding. The quality of the plumage should be close and firm in texture to give an all-important clean-cut outline to the bird.

Being such a heavily built bird the Norwich has not the agility and liveliness of some of the smaller breeds of canary but it should still move around quite freely without any suggestion of sluggishness.

The history of the Scotch Fancy dates from the early part of the nineteenth century when it was developed from imported stock of Belgian origin during the 1820s and 1830s. By late Victorian times it had achieved considerable popularity among Scottish fanciers, particularly in the Glasgow area, but since then it has been on the decline and today is a very rare breed.

The Scotch Fancy is one of the old-time 'birds of position' with a special type of posture that shows off its points to full advantage. It holds itself erect with its body in the form of a long and tapering curve, the head being thrust forward with the neck extended and the tail sweeping well under the perch to complete the crescent-shaped outline. It should also show plenty of life and action, with a bold and jaunty carriage when travelling from perch to perch of its show cage. The standard size is $6\frac{3}{4}$ in. but few of the remaining Scotch Fancies of the present day quite measure up to that. This is another of the old breeds of canary which is in the hands of a few dedicated admirers who are working to try to halt the decline and are attempting to re-establish it in the canary fancy.

The Yorkshire is a comparatively late arrival on the scene in the canary world, its first official standard having been drawn up in 1894. It was originally a 'manufactured' breed assembled by crossings involving the native common canary of the county with the Lancashire plainhead, the old-time Norwich, and the Belgian canary. The final outcome has resulted in one of the most popular breeds of the present century and also one of the most distinctive. It is now the only widely bred example of a group of varieties known collectively as 'birds of position' in which the ability to

Scots Fancy

Yorkshire

stand up and hold a posture in the show cage is an important feature. The Yorkshire is a long and elegant bird averaging about $6\frac{3}{4}$ in. in length, although many of the finest specimens well exceed this. It stands in an erect attitude, with fearless carriage, its legs being quite long, yet without having the appearance of being stilty. Its body shows a perfect tapering off from shoulders to tail, with close, short, and tight feathering to emphasize this contour. The wings and tail are proportionately long, well braced, and closely folded. Although colour has not the same importance as in the Norwich, it should be pure and level throughout and should receive the assistance of colour feeding during the moult.

Because of the importance of position, the Yorkshire needs more than the usual attention in show training, to which the fancier must be prepared to spend a fair amount of time if he is to succeed in close competition.

Continental Type Breeds. The Continental breeds tend to fall into two groups, 'posture' canaries and 'frilled' canaries, although some, in fact, combine these two characteristics. Historically they all appear to have had a common origin in an old Dutch breed of canary in the eighteenth century, but during the nineteenth century various local developments took place in different parts of the continent which have resulted in the breeds of the present day.

One of the very oldest and most famous of these breeds is the Belgian (known on the Continent as the *Bossu Belge*, or *Belgische Bult*, meaning 'Belgian Humpback') which at one time was much esteemed by fanciers, both for its own sake and for its value in crossing with other breeds to bring about an improvement in such qualities as style, posture, and refinement. With the gradual decline in the popularity of the older fancy breeds of canary, the Belgian, in common with several others, lost favour, and the two World Wars fought across its homeland reduced still further its numbers : today it is in very few hands, even in Belgium itself. Furthermore, the breed of today shows some degeneration, both in type and size, compared with its condition in its heyday.

The great feature which distinguishes the Belgian from all other canaries is its high, prominent shoulders which provide its remarkable hump-backed appearance. It is also notable as being the foremost of all the 'birds of position' and can take up its striking pose in the show cage, whenever required to do so, by gripping the perch firmly and pulling itself up to its fullest possible height. At this point the line of the back, from the shoulders to the tip of the tail, should be completely perpendicular — this being an essential feature of a show Belgian — and, at the same time, the head is actually depressed, with the neck stretching out to its full limit and the beak pointing towards the floor of the cage so that the outline of the bird bears some resemblance to a figure seven.

What the crested head is to certain English breeds, so the frilled characteristic is to several Continental 'frilled' varieties. As its name implies, the principal feature of these breeds is the curling, or frilling, of the feathers into a distinctive formation which is basically the same in each case. There is a 'mantle' which is formed by the feathers on the back being divided by a central parting and then curling round over each shoulder like a cape. There is the 'jabot' which is formed by the breast feathers curling inwards to meet in the centre in the form of a closed shell, or frilly shirt-front. And there are the 'fins' which are formed by bunches of feathers just above the thighs which sweep outwards and upwards around the wings.

Belgian Fancy

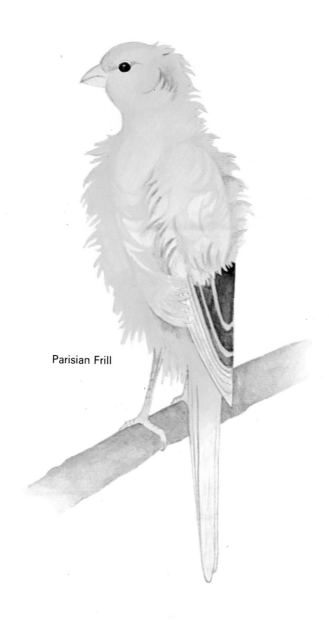

Parisian Frill

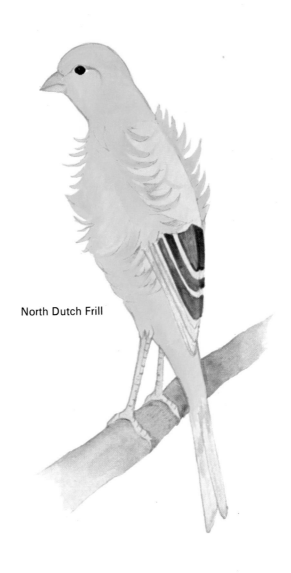

North Dutch Frill

Since each of the breeds possesses these basic frills such differences as exist between them are in the nature of size and stance, density and amount of feathering, and the possession of additional frills to those described above.

The breed in which all of these characteristics are most highly developed is the Parisian Frill (*Frisé Parisien*) which also has the distinction of being the largest — $7\frac{1}{2}$–8 in. according to the official standard. It is obviously a well-built bird, distinguished by the length of its body, the density and quantity of its frilling, and its well-poised carriage. In addition to the main frills, it has curled feathers upon its head, neck, and face, a general collar of frilled feathers, the mantle continuing well down the back to the rump, and covert feathers falling away on either side of the base of the tail in a similar manner to those of a cockerel.

The North Dutch Frill (*Frisé Hollandais du Nord*) may at first sight be taken for a smaller version of the Parisian, but a closer inspection will reveal otherwise, for it has several features that differ in detail from those of the larger breed. The North Dutch, apart from being smaller (about $6\frac{3}{4}$ in.), is much less densely feathered. Too heavy a frilling, in fact, is a fault and greater importance is attached to the correctness, regularity, and symmetry of the frills. It has a small, neat head without any frills and a neck clearly visible from among the body frills, and itself free from frilling. The lower part of the body (rump, vent, thighs, etc.) should also be free from frills and the bird should stand well up on long legs, showing plenty of thigh.

The South Dutch Frill (*Frisé Hollandais du Sud*), in spite of its name, does not hail from the south of Holland but, rather, is the development of the Dutch Frill which took place in Italy. It is more lightly frilled than the North Dutch and, in addition to being a frilled breed of canary, is also a 'bird of position' and can adopt a show position rather like the Belgian but, instead of having a straight back, this is somewhat curved in the manner of the Scotch Fancy. This breed has now become rather scarce, even in its own country.

Another creation of Italian fanciers is the Italian Humpback Frill (the *Gibber italicus*) which is somewhat similar to the previously mentioned breed although much smaller in size. Apart from its small, light frame, it has short, crisp, scanty plumage which results in two of the distinguishing features of the breed, namely, a naked breastbone and thighs bare of feathers. This, too, is a 'posture' canary and holds itself in the form of a figure seven.

South Dutch Frill

Humpbacked Frill

In addition to these there are several other local breeds of frilled canaries. As in the case of the English type breeds, in the Continental varieties colour is generally only of secondary importance and the birds may be clear, ticked, variegated, or green (*see* chapter on Breeding).

Colour Varieties. In a sense fanciers have always been interested in the colour of their canaries, ever since the time that Hervieux produced his list of varieties in 1709. Colour breeding in its modern connotation, however, is a pursuit of the present century and is concerned with the many developments that have occurred in recent years. Colour breeders have concentrated upon this aspect of canary culture alone and have not attempted to standardize their birds into any particular type, so that, in general, the new colour varieties are nonedescript in appearance and not unlike the ordinary wild canary in size and shape.

Apart from the cinnamon mutation which has been present in canaries for at least 250 years, the first new colour to come to the notice of fanciers was the Dilute which appeared in the year 1900. In its original form it occurred as dilute green but, because of its simple mode of inheritance, it has since been allied to the whole range of self colours to give dilute cinnamon, dilute blue, dilute fawn, and so on. The effect of the mutation is to reduce all of the dark pigmentation to something like half of its normal intensity.

White canaries have been reported from time to time throughout the bird's history, but it is only during the present century that they have been permanently established. There are two distinct mutations, the Dominant White and the Recessive White, which are quite different genetically. The dominant white has now been bred into most of the standard type breeds of canary so that it is not unusual to see white Borders, white Glosters, white Frilled canaries, and so on, at shows today. The recessive white, however, is much rarer and is more truly the preserve of the colour breeder. In the white canaries dark pigmentation occurs as blue, instead of the green of normal yellow canaries, and fawn instead of cinnamon.

By far the most important of the new colour varieties is the Red Factor which has now achieved the status of a major exhibition breed in its own right. This variety owes its origin to experimental breeding undertaken in the hope of producing a red canary. Work on the project began in the 1920s after the discovery that male hybrids between the Hooded Siskin (a brilliant vermilion bird) and the canary frequently proved to be fertile and it was hoped that it would be a simple matter to transfer the supposed 'red factor' from the siskin to the canary. In spite of half a century of useful progress, a genuine red true-breeding variety has failed to materialize. However, aided by special feeding with canthaxanthin during the moult, some very deep red-orange coloured birds can be produced and they form the basis for competition at the shows.

White

Red Factor – red-orange

Pastel

This section of the fancy has also had most of the other colour mutations successfully incorporated into the breed, many of which are, visually, extremely attractive.

The Pastel mutation, which has occurred since the Second World War, is also a most attractive colour form. It affects the lipochrome (ground) colour of the canary by producing a dilution and levelling out the pigment throughout the plumage giving, as its name implies, a delightful 'pastel' effect rather than the normal, deeper tone. In yellow birds this colour is of a primrose shade and is called ivory pastel, while in Red Factors it is a pale shade of rose pink called rose pastel. Once again, in combination with some of the other mutations, some very beautiful colour effects are produced.

Even more recently, in 1960, another type of pastel mutation occurred, this time affecting the melanin (black and brown) pigments, so that it is known as the Melanin Pastel. Its effect is roughly the same as the previously mentioned mutation insofar as it dilutes and levels out the pigments — especially in the case of the cinnamon, where even the pencilling on the feathers disappears, leaving a uniform light-brown colour throughout.

The Opal mutation is yet another which affects the melanin pigments by way of dilution. It differs from the old dilute and from the melanin pastel both visually and in its mode of inheritance.

Several other interesting new mutations, which show considerable promise for the future, have occurred on the Continent in recent years. These include the Ino series, in which all birds have red eyes, and the Greywings. Regrettably, nomenclature in the field of colour breeding is still somewhat confused, the various mutations sometimes being known by different names in different countries, but standardization is bound to come now that there is an overall authority, the 'Confédération Ornithologique Mondiale'.

Ino

Singing Canaries. Male canaries of all breeds are, of course, capable of song, and most people are quite satisfied with what, to them, is a pleasing, tuneful, and cheerful performance. To the true connoisseur, however, there is only one breed of real class in this respect and that is the Roller canary. This canary differs from all the breeds previously described, which are essentially visual in their appeal: it is bred exclusively for its singing qualities. This specialized branch of the hobby originated during the eighteenth century in the Hartz Mountains of Germany and was particularly centred in St Andreasburg which, like Norwich in Britain, became one of the great centres of canary culture in Europe.

It was discovered at quite an early stage that canaries were capable of imitating the songs of other birds, and accomplished vocalists, such as the nightingale and woodlark, were often made use of as 'tutors' for young canaries that were just starting to sing. Later on, musical instruments like the flute were employed in a similar manner, until ultimately a device known as a 'bird organ' was developed, able to produce continuous rolling, trilling, and bubbling notes for the young canaries to copy. It is the continuous rolling delivery of the song that gives the breed its popular name.

Various passages known as 'tours', can readily be recognized by anyone with a good musical ear, since each differs in tone, pitch, and mode of delivery. They have been given distinctive names, such as 'Hollow Roll', 'Bass Roll', 'Bell Roll', 'Water Roll', 'Glucke', 'Water Glucke', 'Glucke Roll', 'Flutes', 'Schockel', 'Bell', 'Hollow Bell', and 'Deep Bubbling Water', and they form the bases of competition at shows where the birds are marked on a points scale according to the excellence of their delivery of each of these tours.

Although Rollers are quite attractive little birds, they do not have much to recommend them in the way of type or colour. It is, per-haps, inevitable that attempts have been made from time to time to combine the Roller's song with the qualities of a better type of bird. This has happened in the case of the American Singer in the U.S.A. and, more recently, in the Irish Fancy, but it must be said at once that results are disappointing as these breeds tend to be neither one thing nor the other, although quite useful as house-hold songsters.

American Breeds. The canary fancy in the Americas, both North and South, has tended to follow the pattern of that in Continental Europe, that is to say the majority of fanciers favouring either Rollers, or, for colour breeding, Red Factors. There is a small following, too, for the type breeds, especially the English varieties —

Roller (variegated)

in North America — and the Continental ones — in South America. Neither continent has yet produced any outstanding breeds of its own.

With so many different breeds of canary from which to make a choice, the beginner frequently seeks the advice of the expert to guide him. Some of the more highly developed 'fancy' varieties are a little more difficult to raise than the commoner breeds so that there may be something to be said in favour of 'getting one's hand in' for a year or so with an easier variety. In the end the true enthusiast will go in for the variety to which he is most attracted, whether it is alleged to be difficult or not, and it must be admitted that success is much more likely to follow 'where the heart is'.

43

Cages and equipment

To many people the only place for keeping birds is in an aviary in which the inmates have complete freedom of flight. Canaries can certainly be kept in such conditions, either by themselves or associated with other finches, where they will add to the attractions of any garden by their colour and song. Providing the owner has no ambitions on the show bench, a great deal of pleasure can be gained from keeping the birds in this way, especially if the stock consists of some of the more brightly-hued of the colour varieties or even of a crossbred collection of singing canaries.

Serious breeding cannot be expected in an aviary where control cannot be exercised over the activities of the birds, who are prone to choose their own mates rather than those that the fancier had planned for them! The only really satisfactory method of breeding exhibition canaries is in cages where they can be kept under complete control at all times, and cages therefore are a major and important item of the birdkeeper's equipment. Many old manuals on the subject illustrated various types of cage that were in use by fanciers in former days, but experience shows that nowadays a simple basic design is the best and cheapest way of housing the stock. It is readily adaptable to all phases of the hobby, with the sole exception of exhibiting, where custom dictates that special cages are required for each of the different breeds.

The simple, general-purpose cage is commonly known in the fancy as a 'double breeder', and it is the most widely used because it combines a reasonable size with ease in handling. It can be divided by a moveable partition into two separate compartments if required, or left open to its full length to make a single large cage. As its name implies, it is used in the appropriate season as a breeding unit, usually for one pair of canaries and their young brood before weaning, but at other times, as a stock cage, it can accommodate either two adult cock birds or a small group of three or four hens. Growing youngsters in small groups, prior to sexing and moulting, can also be suitably housed so that the 'double breeder' finds employment throughout the year as a convenient general utility unit.

These cages can be bought ready made and completely fitted out from suppliers of fanciers' equipment, but many people prefer to make their own, which is quite a simple matter, and also saves money. Basically the cage is box shaped, with wooden sides, top, bottom, and back, only the fronts being made of wire. A normal

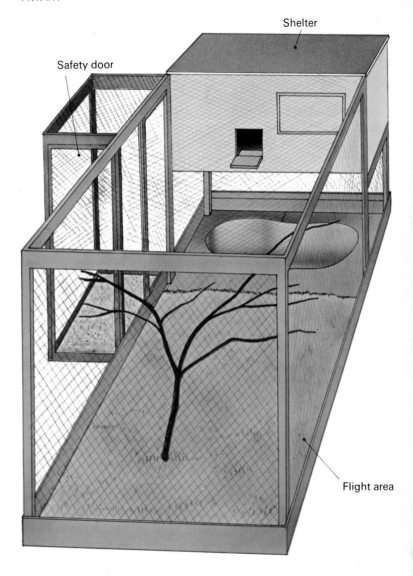

Safety door

Shelter

Flight area

size is 36 in. in length, 16 in. in height, and 10 in. in depth, the actual dimensions depending upon whether the larger or smaller breeds are being kept. If several cages are made, it is wise to keep to a standard pattern throughout so that they will be easily interchangeable if the need arises.

The wood used in the construction of cages is generally $\frac{3}{8}$ in. thick, with the exception of the backs which may be of plywood or hardboard, but many modern composition materials may be equally suitable provided that they are not of a porous nature which might possibly harbour insect pests. All joints should fit well, preferably glued and screwed to prevent any gaps subsequently opening up, and all surfaces should be sandpapered smooth.

Very few fanciers nowadays make their own wire cage-fronts, since they can be quite cheaply bought in a whole range of sizes. To support the fronts in position an additional strip of wood is required across the whole length of the front of the cage and another is needed from front to back in order to carry the sliding partition. The only other items needed are the cleaning trays for the bottom of the cage. These should slide freely in and out and may be constructed from sheet metal or wood since either is satisfactory.

A plastic emulsion paint is the best for the interior finish of the cage; it is quick-drying and its lack of odour renders it superior to gloss paints or enamels, and regular repainting can be carried out as necessary, with little disturbance to the birds. A very pale colour is recommended in order to keep the cages as light as possible within, but the exteriors may be finished according to choice. Paints containing a lead base should never be used.

As an alternative to having separate cages, a built-in system can be used, based upon similar principles to the built-in furniture so frequently constructed by handymen today. Such a system of caging can be perfectly satisfactory but has the disadvantage that it does not allow the removal of individual cages if for any reason they need special attention in the way of cleaning, disinfecting, or repainting. But with careful management and close observance of the principles of hygiene no problems should normally be encountered.

Regardless of the purpose for which cages are being used at any given time, standard fittings will consist of perches, seed hoppers, and drinking vessels, all of which can be purchased from the usual fanciers' suppliers. Perches of course can be readily made at home

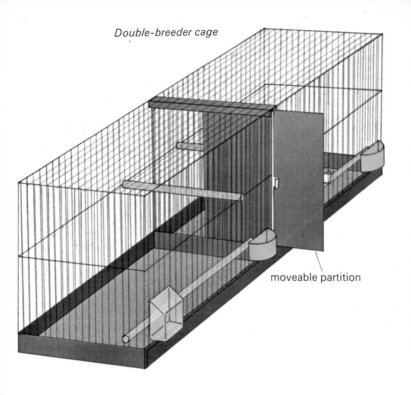

Double-breeder cage

moveable partition

home-made cage

moveable partition

47

and it is a useful plan to have plenty of spare sets so that clean ones are always available. They should be made of white softwood and can be purchased in a variety of sizes and shapes suitable for the type and age of bird being accommodated at the time. Varying the sizes of perch also gives some exercise to the gripping mechanism of the birds' feet. As a general guide they may be round, oval, square, or rectangular in section and may vary from about $\frac{3}{8}$ in. to $\frac{3}{4}$ in. in width.

Since they will need to be removed for regular cleaning, the perches should not be made a permanent fixture. Various simple methods of fixing them can be employed, the most common being by means of a small panel pin at the back and a vertical notch at the front, or by using a perch holder which will twist securely between the wires of the cage front. Whichever method is used it is important to see that they are firmly fastened.

The usual seed hoppers in use today are made of transparent plastic which, being pressed in one piece, have smooth surfaces and rounded corners so that they are easy to clean and have no awkward places where dust and dirt may collect. The most popular drinking vessels are the simple open-topped glass variety, which again are quick and easy to clean. Vessels with covered tops, which are often supplied with fancy drawing-room cages, are less suitable, being a little more awkward to clean out, and those made from plastic, although quite suitable in general use, tend to become stained in time, especially if medicines or tonics have been administered in them.

Even before purchasing or constructing the cages, the canary fancier will need to give some thought as to where they are to be accommodated. Canaries are most adaptable creatures and have been successfully bred in all kinds of places but better results are much more likely if they can be given a room of their own. In such a room quietness and lack of disturbance during the all-important breeding season are often key factors that make the difference between failure and success. Rooms that are specially given over to the hobby are known to fanciers as 'birdrooms' and are usually either a shed-like structure erected in the back yard or garden, or a spare-room conversion within the home. Either has its own particular advantages and disadvantages but whichever of the two types may finally be employed there are certain basic requirements needed to make them suitable for birdkeeping. Among the most important points to watch is that the birdroom should be free from damp, draughts, bad ventilation, and widely fluctuating tempera-

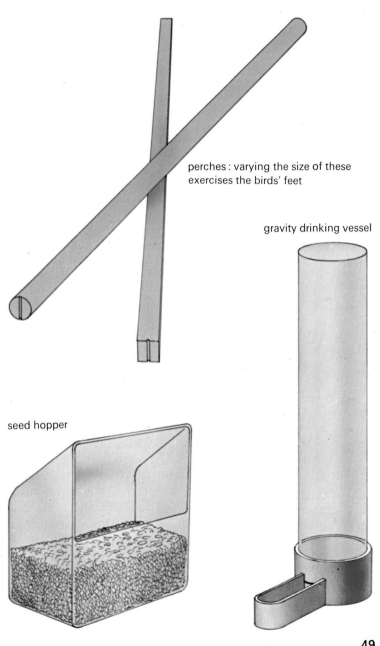

perches : varying the size of these
exercises the birds' feet

gravity drinking vessel

seed hopper

49

tures, all of which are conditions contrary to the wellbeing of canaries.

Quite often very little needs to be done in the way of adapting an indoor room for canary keeping, the most obvious being the provision of some staging on which to stand the cages. As a safeguard against the loss of any bird that may escape from its cage, the windows should be covered with small-mesh wire-netting. Some arrangement should also be made to prevent seed husks and feathers from blowing under the door and so becoming a nuisance elsewhere. If there is any choice in the matter, a room in a quiet part of the house should prove ideal, especially if it has an easterly or south-easterly aspect, with the resulting benefit of the early morning sunshine. At the same time a room facing a busy road is best avoided since any street lights shining in at night, and the headlamps of passing cars, would prove disturbing to the birds and might well be the cause of unsuccessful breeding results.

Although a birdroom within the house has the decided advantage of convenience, most fanciers prefer to have an outdoor room for their hobby, and in most cases this is the only possible way for them to keep birds. An outdoor birdroom need be nothing more elaborate than a garden shed, but if something more decorative, and in keeping with ornamental garden surroundings, is required there is no limit to what may be done provided expense is no object.

Whether constructing one's own, or purchasing a birdroom ready made, it is wise to have the largest that space and funds will permit, for nothing is more frustrating, after a season or two, than to find that one's hobby has outgrown its accommodation and either an extension has to be built, or an entirely new birdroom considered. As a rough guide, a shed of 8 ft. × 6 ft. × 7 ft. should accommodate up to sixty birds, which would be the equivalent of six breeding pairs and their optimum expected progeny, say eight young per pair, in one season's breeding. Similarly a building of 12 ft. × 8 ft. × 7 ft. would hold up to eighty birds, the outcome of eight breeding pairs in a season. To achieve this the maximum use of the interior space would have to be made by having cages all round three sides of the birdroom and four tiers high, in which case all of the windows plus the door would have to be at the front. Many fanciers prefer to have things slightly less concentrated in order to allow for some cupboards and shelves, for the storage of the many items of equipment which are needed in various phases of the hobby.

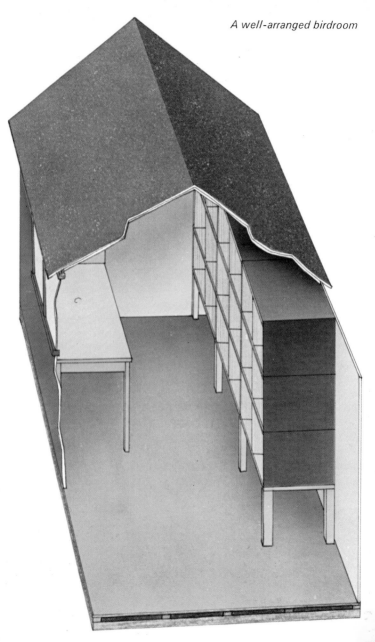

A well-arranged birdroom

The birdroom may be constructed of any of the usual materials employed for outdoor work. A brick building would obviously be very satisfactory but probably far too expensive for most people ; in the main, timber or asbestos-sheeting structures are the most widely used. They should always be lined with some other material, such as plywood or hardboard, and efficiently insulated to avoid fluctuating temperatures. Adequate window space, to ensure that the room is well lit, and efficient ventilators should be incorporated into the design.

The question of the use of artificial lighting and heating will probably arise, and it must be said at once that canaries normally need neither of these, and indeed flourish better without them, but if the fancier's circumstances dictate that he must attend to his birds in the evenings then in winter artificial lighting will become a necessity. Similarly in regions where the winters are more severe, and the birds' water is constantly being frozen, a moderate amount of heat is desirable to prevent this from happening, but temperatures should never be so high as to make the birds soft and unhealthy.

The budding fancier is often in need of some guidance as to what the entire equipment requirements might be for his initial season. Assuming him to be starting off with, say, two pairs of birds, as indeed many beginners do, they would be roughly as follows :

Six double breeding cages, fully equiped with seed hoppers, drinkers, and perches. (Two for the breeding pairs and four for the expected youngsters.) Twelve grit containers. Twelve cuttlefish holders. Six baths. Six nesting pans and linings. Six packets of nesting material. Twelve dummy eggs. Six feeding trays. Six egg-food drawers. A mixing basin and spoon. A seed sieve. A storage bin for seed. All of these items are obtainable from pet stores and fanciers' suppliers and their precise uses will be explained in later chapters.

Management and feeding

The management of canaries covers a wide range of activities which take place throughout the year and embrace all phases of the hobby, but here it is being treated in a more restricted sense to cover those ordinary routine matters not specifically connected with breeding, moulting, or exhibiting. Many of these tasks are of an elementary and repetitive, perhaps even monotonous, nature, but the fancier who carries them out conscientiously will get far more pleasure out of his hobby and will be far more likely to succeed, for it has often been said that success with livestock is in direct proportion to the care and attention they receive.

As far as the general organization of the birdroom goes, the dangers of overcrowding should always be borne in mind and the caging of the birds arranged with a view to avoiding this. It is the usual practice to keep adult cock birds caged singly since they are occasionally inclined to fight, but hens are generally more docile and can safely be kept in small groups. Birds that are intended for exhibition, whatever their sex and age, will need to be kept in separate cages for the duration of the show season. On their own they will keep steadier and there will be less danger of them soiling their plumage, as might be the case if they were associating with others. There is also the added advantage of being able to give them any special treatment in the way of feeding, bathing, and show training that they may need.

Having established a pattern of caging, the fancier should then organize the management of his stock to suit his own particular circumstances and endeavour to keep to a routine that will ensure that all eventualities are regularly dealt with. The larger the number of birds being kept the more obvious will be the need for a set routine.

The various jobs to be done can be divided into daily, weekly, and occasional tasks. The ordinary daily procedure is nothing more than feeding and watering the birds, which can be done in the morning or evening. All seed hoppers will need to have the loose husks on the surface blown away and then be topped up with fresh seed, and the water vessels will have to be emptied, wiped clean, and then refilled with fresh water. If any extra food is being given, such as greenstuff or softfood, this can also be attended to at this time.

The biggest weekly task to be tackled is the cleaning out of the birds' cages and this is usually coupled with allowing them to

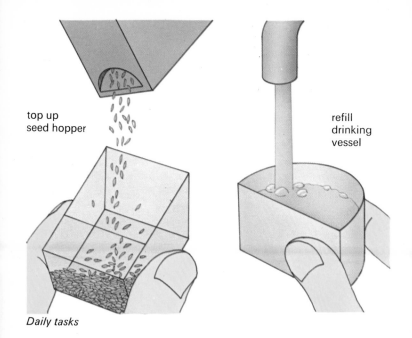

top up
seed hopper

refill
drinking
vessel

Daily tasks

bathe. Canaries like to indulge in bathing at almost any time, but they do make a lot of mess in the process: unless one is prepared to mop up after them, it is more convenient to introduce the bath cages just prior to the weekly clean out.

The practical value of double breeders is again apparent when cages are being cleaned, for it is a simple matter to run the birds into one half of the cage while the opposite side is being dealt with and the process then reversed. If the wire fronts are easily detachable they should each be removed in turn to allow the inside of the cage to be wiped clean and dry. Clean sets of perches can then be inserted and the soiled ones set aside for washing later in hot water to which a little mild antiseptic solution has been added. Care should be taken never to treat perches with strong disinfectants otherwise sore feet and eyes are likely to follow. The trays on the floor of the cage should be withdrawn, emptied of their soiled contents, and then replaced. Many kinds of litter have been used for covering these trays but the fancier's choice almost invariably tends to be coarse-cut sawdust which is clean and absorbent and ideal for the purpose. Other substances include

54

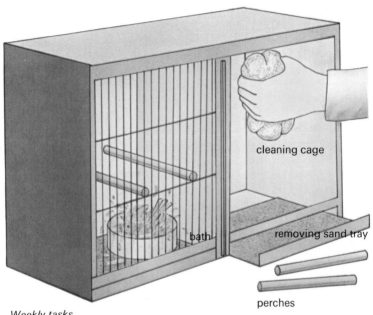

cleaning cage

bath

removing sand tray

perches

Weekly tasks

sand, clean newspaper, thick blotting paper and sanded paper, but these may need changing more frequently than once a week.

Other weekly tasks to be carried out are replenishing the grit containers, sifting the seed from the hoppers, and washing out the drinking vessels. Although the latter have been wiped clean daily it is still advisable to give them a wash once a week in hot water to make sure that they are thoroughly clean and that no germs are present. Grit, which is essential to a bird's digestive system, must always be available, and the grit containers will need to be topped up once a week and occasionally emptied and washed before filling with fresh grit. The seed hoppers, although they have had the husks blown from them each day, will be found after a time to contain all kinds of other debris which will need to be sifted and removed during the weekly cleaning out. This can be accomplished quite easily with a small-mesh kitchen sieve if only small quantities are involved, but some fanciers will need a much larger utensil if the task is not to take up an inordinate amount of time. Some birds by habit are very wasteful, scattering uneaten seed about, but there is no need for this to be thrown away as it can be cleaned and sifted along with the other seed and returned to the hoppers after these have been wiped clean.

A few weeks before the beginning of the breeding season it is advisable to have a thorough overhaul and spring cleaning of the birdroom, cages, and equipment, for once the birds have started to breed they should be disturbed as little as possible. During this spring cleaning the fabric of the birdroom can be attended to and any minor repairs and redecorating done while the cages are removed for their annual overhaul. This overhaul should include a thorough washing, disinfecting, drying, and repainting; even though the cages may be in no apparent need of such treatment, it is better to start the season with everything in really good order.

At the close of the year's breeding activities it is also a good plan to give similar treatment once more to those cages which have actually been occupied by the breeding pairs, and, at the same time, to cleanse and disinfect all items of special equipment that have been used for breeding and which will not be required again until the following year.

Although the birds may be ideally housed in their birdroom and cages, this is still only part of the way towards success, for it is probably true to say that the single most important factor in the management of stock is correct feeding. It is usual nowadays to purchase seeds and various supplementary food items from bird-food specialists who have the resources to place on the market products of the highest quality, but the serious fancier should still endeavour to learn all he can about the principles of feeding. In so doing, rather than a mere routine supplying of seeds and foods, he will have an underlying knowledge of what is involved and be able to adjust his feeding to the individual requirements of his birds at different seasons of the year.

It is probably generally known that the basic food materials are classified as proteins, carbohydrates, fats, and oils, and that most items of food usually contain one or more of these. In the case of the seeds that are commonly fed to canaries they all contain varying proportions of each of these substances so that the birds are unlikely ever to suffer from an actual shortage of any particular item, but the more important problem is that of correct balance. Although the requirements of canaries do not appear to have received any detailed scientific investigation, in the commercial world of poultry keeping it has been determined that the balance of daily rations should be in the proportion of one part protein to four and a half parts carbohydrates and oils, and it is probable that

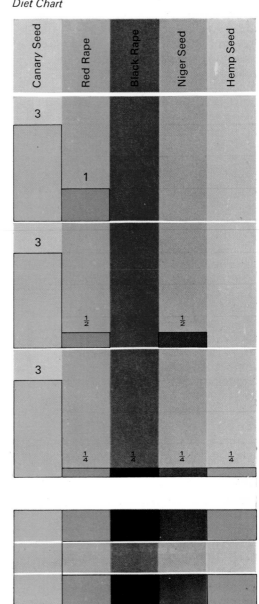

Three alternative methods of mixing seeds to ensure a healthy diet

Diet Chart

Canary Seed | Red Rape | Black Rape | Niger Seed | Hemp Seed

Suggested diet 1

Suggested diet 2

Suggested diet 3

Protein

Carbohydrates

Oil

this is a fairly constant figure for all seed-eating birds.

From the point of view of the practical canary fancier this usually means a staple mixture consisting of three parts of canary seed and one part of red rape seed; but other variations such as three parts canary seed to one half part red rape seed and one half part niger seed, or three parts canary seed to a quarter part red rape seed, a quarter part black rape seed, a quarter part niger seed, and a quarter part hemp seed, are also quite frequently used. It should perhaps be explained here that the 'canary seed' referred to is not a mixture of seeds in a packet, but a definite species of plant (*Phalaris canariensis*), whose seed is the 'bread and butter' of the canary and forms its major item of diet.

This important seed consists mainly of carbohydrates, but with a fair percentage of protein and a little oil. The only other seed of a somewhat similar nature, occasionally used by canary breeders, is groats. Rape seed, niger, hemp, linseed, and mawseed are mainly oily seeds, also containing a fair proportion of protein, but as birds do not appear to need large amounts of oil, overfeeding with these seeds should be avoided.

Fanciers also make use of a mixture of seeds called Condition Seed; as its name suggests, it is a useful aid to fitness for birds slightly below par and for bringing stock into peak condition for breeding or show season. Keen fanciers, if they are able, will also provide their birds with various kinds of wild seeds that are normally eaten by native finches; these often make a welcome change from the standard dry-seed mixtures. Care must be taken that they have not been gathered from areas where agricultural sprays have been employed.

Apart from seeds, two other important parts of the canary's diet consist of greenfood and softfood. The former is a useful source of vitamins and is usually offered twice a week throughout the winter months, gradually increasing to every other day, and finally to daily at the start of the breeding season. A wide variety of green-stuff is generally available at most times, ranging from garden produce such as lettuce, Brussels sprouts, kale, celery, and savoy cabbage to greengrocers' items such as watercress, chicory, endive, and mustard and cress, and wild plants such as groundsel and dandelion. If nothing green is available a slice of sweet apple or some shredded carrot is usually appreciated.

Under the heading of softfood come two well-tried items used by canary breeders. The first is a kind of fine biscuit meal, with additives such as dried egg, powdered milk, wheat-germ meal, dried yeast, and vitamin and mineral supplements; this is used as a rearing food for young canaries and is also fed to adult stock at special times of the year. The second 'soft' food is bread and milk to which some fanciers are addicted during the breeding season but many others prefer to restrict its use to medicinal purposes: it has a strong laxative effect!

As was suggested earlier, mere routine feeding of the birds without understanding is hardly to be recommended, but a beginner will need some guidance in the matter and for his assistance the following suggestions are made:

1 *November and December.* In the seed hoppers a mixture consisting of three parts canary seed and one part red rape seed. Extras: Sunday — Softfood; Monday — Greenstuff; Wednesday — Condition Seed; Friday — Greenstuff.

2 *January.* Remember that conditioning for the breeding season is a gradual process and starts early. In the seed hoppers a mixture consisting of three parts canary seed, one half part red rape seed and one half part niger seed. Extras: Sunday — Softfood; Monday — Greenstuff; Wednesday — Condition Seed; Thursday — Greenstuff; Saturday — Condition Seed.

3 *February.* Seed mixture for the seed hoppers as before. Extras: Sunday — Softfood; Monday — Greenstuff; Wednesday — Condition Seed; Thursday — Softfood; Friday — Greenstuff; Saturday — Condition Seed.

4 *March.* Seed mixture for the seed hoppers as before. Extras: Sunday — Softfood with hard-boiled egg; Monday — Greenstuff; Tuesday — Condition Seed; Wednesday — Greenstuff; Thursday — Softfood and Condition Seed; Friday — Greenstuff; Saturday — Condition Seed.

This gradual run up to the breeding season should bring the birds quite naturally, and without forcing, into proper condition. Feeding during the breeding and moulting seasons, which cover the remainder of the year, is covered in other chapters.

Breeding

It is usually the ultimate ambition of every newcomer to the canary fancy to possess a strain of birds of his own which are true to standard and successful in competition, but often at the outset he is quite happy to breed a few canaries of any sort, good, bad, or indifferent. While in no way decrying this attitude, and at the same time admitting the value of 'getting one's hand in' with inexpensive stock, it must be pointed out that good birds take no more time, trouble, or expense to look after than mediocre ones. The difference is only in the initial outlay: the beginner is urged to acquire as soon as possible as good a foundation stock as he can afford.

This is not to say that he needs to spend vast sums of money. High prices have of course been paid from time to time for birds of outstanding merit, as is the case in most branches of livestock keeping, but good, reliable breeding stock is obtainable at quite reasonable prices from most well-established fanciers, who are usually only too willing to help a newcomer to get started in the hobby. They will often supply not only properly matched pairs for the first breeding season, but also give useful advice on the subsequent selection to be made from among the progeny.

For the fancier who has progressed beyond these initial stages the breeding season presents the interesting annual challenge of maintaining the high quality of his stock, and even improving upon it if he can. This he must do by the skilful selection of his breeding pairs each season, basing his judgement upon the standard of excellence of his particular breed, as drawn up by the specialist societies, by a visual comparison of his own and other fanciers' birds, usually best accomplished on the show bench, and by reference to the bird's own pedigree and the recorded performance of its nearest relatives. It is always advisable to be quite critical in one's selection and to be ready to reject unsuitable birds, always remembering that better progress will be achieved with a few really good pairs than with a great many moderate ones.

Before tackling the job of selection in any detail there are certain essentials that need to be observed and the first of these concerns the colours and markings common to most breeds of canary. There are two distinct qualities of feather to be found in each breed, known to fanciers as 'yellow' and 'buff', and it is almost invariably the practice to make up a pair from one of each kind. It makes no difference which of the pair is the yellow and which is the buff (it may be a yellow cock mated to a buff hen, or vice versa),

Original bird

for the result is always the same: that is, about half of each colour type among the progeny.

To distinguish between these two colours is a relatively simple matter despite the fact that both of them are actually yellow birds. In the 'yellow' the colouring pigment extends completely over the whole web of the feather, whereas in the 'buff' it stops just short of the outer margin, leaving a thin edging of white. The general effect of this is to produce a lightly frosted appearance covering the yellow so that buff birds appear to be slightly paler than the yellows. Of further significance to fanciers is the fact that there is an actual structural difference between the two types of feather, the buff being slightly larger, broader, and softer in texture than the yellow. The result is that, all other things being equal, a buff bird appears to be rather bolder in appearance than a yellow — a fact that has some importance in certain breeds where yellows may be at some disadvantage upon the show bench.

The next point for consideration in the selection of breeding pairs concerns the presence or absence of dark pigmentation in the plumage. Before its domestication the canary was entirely a dark-plumaged bird, caused by two melanin pigments (brown and black) being superimposed upon a plain yellow background, or ground, colour. This combination is still commonly found in the bird today and is known to fanciers as 'self green'. The complete absence of any dark pigmentation of course leaves only the yellow ground colour present: the familiar clear-yellow canary.

In between the two extremes are to be found a wide range of markings of a more or less pied, or mottled, nature, varying from a bird quite lightly marked to a very heavily marked one, all of which are referred to as 'variegated' birds. For convenience of reference even these are further subdivided and given technical names such as 'ticked', 'lightly marked', 'heavily variegated', 'three-parts dark', 'foul green', and various other categories.

In breeding most of the 'type' canaries the fancier can make up his pairs entirely ignoring the markings, but it is more usual to try to keep a balance so that he has reasonable numbers of each category from which to select show specimens for the various classes. To this end it is useful to bear in mind that, in general, clear mated to clear will give mostly clear youngsters. Green × green will similarly give mostly green young. Clear × green will produce mainly variegated young, and two variegated birds mated together will produce mostly variegated youngsters, but may well 'throw' occasional clears and greens as well. All of these are given for general guidance only, to help the beginner know what he may expect, but obviously much would depend upon the antecedents of the birds in question.

In many of the breeds of canary, white varieties are also to be found. These are birds in which the yellow ground colour is suppressed by a 'dominant white' genetical factor so that in the clear form they are white instead of the normal yellow. Pigmentation in this case appears as a slate blue so that the self-coloured bird is referred to as a 'blue' and the variegated as a 'blue variegated white'. When breeding for these colours it is usual to make up a pair of one white-ground parent and one ordinary yellow-ground parent, and the expectation of this mating is 50 per cent of each colour variety among the progeny. There is no advantage to be gained in mating two white birds together since they do not produce any more whites than the other mating and, in fact, fewer youngsters altogether owing to the existence of a genetically lethal factor which prevents 25 per cent of the chicks from surviving. The actual expectation is 50 per cent whites, 25 per cent normal yellows and 25 per cent non-viable 'double-factor' dominant whites.

These facts are not true in the case of the 'recessive white' canary which is a different mutation and does breed true when mated white $\times$ white. Birds of this kind are relatively scarce and are mainly confined to the realms of colour breeding rather than to the 'type' breeds.

The various crested breeds of canary present a similar 'problem' to that of the dominant white, insofar as the mutation that gave rise to the crested characteristic is also a dominant factor that is lethal when present in a double dose. It is therefore generally unwise to mate two crested birds together, and the standard practice is to make up a pair of one crested parent and one plain-head of the same breed.

Having mastered these few 'basics' in canary culture the fancier can then set about the final selection of his breeding pairs and his first criterion should always be that of physical fitness. However desirable a bird may be in other respects, if it is at all suspect on the grounds of health it should be discarded at once. Even if such a bird breeds successfully it may well be laying the foundations for a weak and debilitated stock that could cause endless trouble later on. Secondly, the breeder should bring his judgement to bear, as was explained earlier in the chapter, by applying both a visual standard and referring to his records. In doing this he must be firm

Clear Yellow

in rejecting any bird that shows serious defects, for once these get into a strain they generally prove difficult to eradicate. Few birds of course are perfect and he will have to accept minor faults for what they are and try as time goes on to eliminate them and so improve his stock.

It is the usual practice among breeders to mate their two best birds together, providing that the circumstances of colour and relationship will allow, and to back these up with the second best pair and so on throughout the stock. By doing this each year and systematically carrying out a rigorous selection programme a high standard can be maintained. It is never advisable to try to 'balance things up' by mating good birds with inferior ones as this will result in general mediocrity. The only exception to this is where a fancier with only a moderate strain has purchased one or two outstanding individuals to 'up-grade' his stock — a long-term breeding programme which, if properly handled, can bring about a recognizable improvement year by year.

So far in this chapter reference has always been made to 'pairs' of birds for breeding, and this is certainly the most widely accepted system, but there are others. Of these probably the most popular is the use of trios; in this system one cock bird is mated to two hens. This can be successfully achieved in two ways: by allowing him to run with each of his partners for a part of each day if both hens are expected to go to nest simultaneously, or by pairing him to one hen first until she has laid her clutch of eggs and then allowing him with the second hen until she has done the same. The cock bird can then either be returned to his first partner to help in rearing the young, or 'rested' until the hens have raised their broods and are ready for nesting again; and here it should be pointed out that the majority of hens will rear their families just as happily on their own as they will with the assistance of their mates.

It is sometimes asked at what age canaries are ready for breeding and how long they will continue to do so. The answer is that, with few exceptions, they are sufficiently mature in the year following the one in which they themselves were bred. At this stage they are technically referred to as 'unflighted' or 'young' birds. Those that are in their second year or upwards are variously known to fanciers as 'flighted', 'overyear', 'adult', or 'old' birds, and they should continue to breed for an average of four or five years — although it can frequently be much longer. Canaries, in common with other small birds, are nor particularly long-lived creatures, and although any that are kept as pets may well live for ten or a dozen years, those

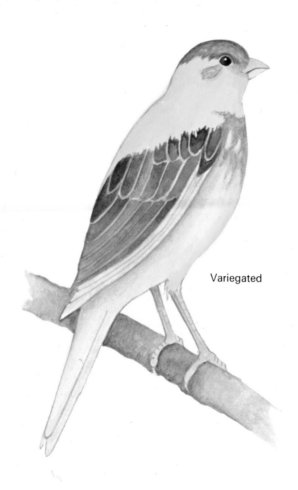

Variegated

used for breeding and exhibition rarely achieve this span.

Before entertaining any thoughts of embarking on the breeding season's activities, the fancier will need to have ready the various specialized items of equipment that will be brought into use, foremost of which will be nest pans and linings. In the confines of a plain wooden cage these pans are necessary for the canary hen to build her nest in; they are made of earthenware, or plastic, and are supplied with wire holders for hanging them onto a hook at the back of the cage. The linings, which are made of felt, become a necessity because some hens are rather slovenly nest-builders and adequate protection is therefore essential for the eggs and young birds. Even for hens that do build well, the lining provides a better foundation than the smooth sides of a nest pan. The actual material supplied for nesting can be purchased from fanciers' sundriesmen, or pet stores, in conveniently sized bags, each containing sufficient for one nest, but the fancier who wishes to provide his own can collect such materials as fine hay, mosses, cowhair, and so on; it would be advisable to sterilize this material before use.

It is the usual practice, when the canary is laying, to remove her eggs each day until the clutch is complete and to substitute dummy ones until she is 'set' to start her incubation. Along with the other items of breeding equipment these dummies can be bought from the usual fanciers' suppliers. A suitable box for holding the real eggs can easily be made and should be provided with sections corresponding to the number of breeding cages in the room so that the various clutches cannot be mixed up. For safety, each section should be lined with some soft material such as cotton wool or flannel.

Special feeding vessels known as egg-food drawers are also necessary to provide the hen with the rearing foods that she will need when she has hatched her brood. These are usually made of plastic and are designed to fit firmly under the cage door. Wooden feeding trays that similarly fit under the door are also very useful, especially when the young birds leave the nest, as they soon learn to feed themselves from these.

To complete his equipment the fancier will also need to provide himself with various kitchen utensils for the preparation of certain rearing foods. The most obvious in this respect will be one or two mixing bowls and spoons, but several large jam jars will be found useful for soaking seed, and a small-meshed sieve will be a necessity for straining the soaked seed and for the processing of

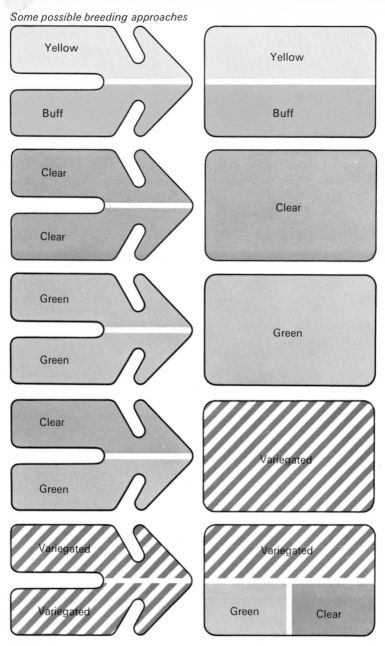

hard-boiled egg if it is decided to use this as an additive to rearing foods. It is also advisable to have a notebook and pencil handy for recording the dates of egg laying, hatching, weaning of chicks, ring numbers, and so on — all of which are necessary to the well-ordered keeping of breeding records.

When all is ready for breeding, the beginner is naturally a little impatient to get started and is frequently tempted to pair his birds up too early. It must be understood that cocks and hens should be kept apart until they are in full breeding condition. To be able to detect just when the time is ripe only comes with experience, and even established fanciers can occasionally err only to find that a hen has laid her eggs before her partner has been introduced.

From early spring onwards the cock birds, if they are fit, will already have been singing vigorously, but with the approach of peak condition the intensity of the song will increase. Then, with head thrown back, dropped wings, body swaying from side to side, and 'marking time' or dancing along the perch, the full-throated courtship song is fairly evident. When not engaged in singing the birds will be trying to gain a view of any hens in nearby cages by putting their heads close to the wires.

Hens, too, will exhibit a marked increase in activity. They will have a general air of restlessness, flying ceaselessly from end to end of their cages, continuing to flap their wings even when stationary, and calling repeatedly to the cock birds. They may be observed carrying pieces of material about in their beaks and may start plucking feathers from their own breasts — a habit which should be discouraged by providing them with a little nesting material to play with. Using this they will probably make preliminary attempts at nest building among the sawdust in the corners of their cages.

Just when the birds will have arrived at this stage of readiness will depend to some extent on their housing and feeding. In most of Britain, and places of similar latitude, the peak is reached early in April, but further south may well be earlier.

During the week or so prior to the expected time for mating the hens should be installed in the cages they will occupy for breeding so that they can become well settled and familiar with their surroundings. The cocks can either be housed in their stock cages or placed in the opposite compartment of the breeding cages to their partners, with the wooden partition between them. As the birds become clearly ripe for breeding a wire slide can be substituted for the wooden one and the birds' reactions noted. If they soon appear to be getting on friendly terms, the slide can be withdrawn

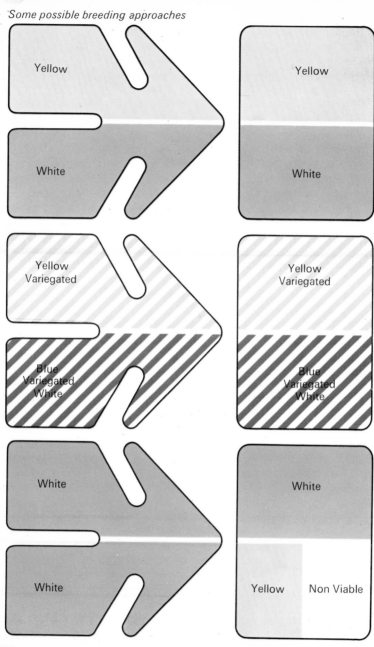

completely to allow them free access to each other. At this stage there may be a little minor squabbling but usually the pair soon settles down peaceably, and within a day or so the nest pan can be introduced.

This is usually hung on the back of the cage so that the rim of the pan is somewhat above the level of the perches but the precise positioning is relatively unimportant. Some hens however are very unpredictable and will insist on ignoring the chosen site and making their nest upon the floor. If this occurs it is preferable to let them have their way and put the nest pan in the position they have chosen. Nesting material can now be supplied, but it will often be found that the hen will merely toy with it for a while before getting down to the more serious business. Some, indeed, are very poor nest builders and fanciers can assist them in their efforts if nothing very substantial has been assembled when egg laying commences.

If the pair was in proper condition at the outset, the first egg should appear within a week after mating. Eggs are laid in the early morning, one every twenty-four hours, until a clutch of four or five has been completed. Most fanciers remove the eggs as laid, substituting them with 'dummy' ones, until the hen has finished her clutch and is ready for incubation. The reason for this procedure is to ensure that the eggs will all hatch at about the same time so that each chick will have an equal start in life.

Before returning the eggs and 'setting' the hen it is advisable to clean out the cage so that she will not be disturbed again during the period of incubation. This normally takes fourteen days, although some hens, particularly of the smaller breeds, will frequently hatch on the thirteenth day. A note should therefore be made of when hatching is to be expected. During incubation the pair can be fed upon a plainer diet than during the days leading up to egg laying, a staple mixture of seed in the hoppers, as for winter feeding, plus a little green food twice weekly being quite adequate. The cock bird, being superfluous at this stage, can either be transferred to a second partner, if double matings are being carried out, or left with his mate to help rear the brood when it hatches.

A sign that hatching has been successfully accomplished will be the appearance of empty egg shells on the floor of the cage and the faint 'cheeping' of the newly-hatched chicks from underneath the hen. Care should be taken not to disturb the birds unduly at this stage: some hens are inclined to be nervous and may possibly

nest pan and holder

nesting materials

egg-food drawer

spoon and jar for mixing foods

seed sieve to remove debris from the food

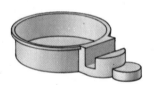

refuse to feed their chicks if interfered with. A quick look, morning and evening, when the hen comes off her nest to feed, is all that the fancier should permit himself in the early days, plus a little unobtrusive observation to ensure that she is feeding her babies satisfactorily.

The young canary is completely dependent upon its parents for the first three weeks of its life so that the breeder is very much in the hands of fate regarding the parental efficiency of his breeding pairs. Fortunately the majority carry out their duties as would be expected, but years of domesticity have produced a small proportion of negligent birds whose offspring may have to be fostered out with other pairs if they are to be successfully reared.

Feeding during the rearing period is of paramount importance, and although there are as many 'systems' as there are fanciers, it will be found that they are almost all variations on a few basic food substances. The main items employed are soft food, soaked seed, greenstuff, and wild seeds, and it is chiefly in method of preparation, quantity, and at what phase they are given that fanciers differ.

As explained in the previous chapter, soft food is an important medium for rearing young canaries and is marketed by several birdfood specialists under trade names. Most of these foods are complete in themselves and merely need to be prepared according to the manufacturers' directions, but some may need the addition of hard-boiled egg to improve the protein content. This can be done by boiling an egg for about ten minutes and then pressing both white and yolk through a small-meshed kitchen sieve. The fine particles of egg thus produced will then easily blend in with the soft food at the rate of about one egg to one cupful of food.

Birdfood specialists also offer mixtures of seeds specially for soaking, but an equal mixture of teazel, rape, and hemp, plus a little canary seed, is usually readily accepted by most hens. It will need soaking for forty-eight hours with a thorough washing and change to fresh water after twenty-four hours, and again another rinsing and draining before being offered to the birds. Fanciers who like to use wild seeds in addition should be guided by the preferences of native finches and gather, as they become ready, chickweed, shepherd's purse, dandelion, and seeding grasses — always providing that they have not been contaminated with agricultural sprays.

Greenstuff that is available during the breeding season is fairly limited in variety and may well be restricted to lettuce or cress,

Nest pan, positioned near, and slightly above, the perch

but in any case many fanciers prefer to offer only small quantities of these materials at this time.

When feeding pairs with newly-hatched young the best course is 'little and often', since, by being given fresh supplies of food, the adult birds are induced to feed the young ones with greater frequency. For the busy fancier, three feeds a day, at morning, midday, and evening, usually prove quite adequate. Although some breeders like to supply all types of rearing food from the moment of hatching, it is more usual to offer egg food only for the first couple of days, adding a little greenstuff and a spray of seeding chickweed from the third day, and soaked seed from the fifth day, so that from then onwards all items are available.

If all goes well the nestlings should develop without any check to their progress right up to the time they are due to leave the nest: usually at twenty-one days. Those that are well advanced may have been hopping about for a day or two before this but they are rarely capable of an independent existence until they are three weeks old. Once the brood has left the nest some fanciers remove them at once to another cage, but others merely separate them from their parents by a wire slide so that the old birds can continue to feed them through the bars until they are observed to be

Softfoods

eggs

Soaked seeds

hemp

red rape seed

canary seed

Greenfoods

cress

Wildseed

shepherd's purse

dandelion

grasses

Suitable foods for young birds

picking up food for themselves.

The newly-weaned chicks should still be fed at least three times daily on the same foods that they have been reared on, and a careful watch kept to ensure that they are all feeding themselves satisfactorily. A wooden feeding tray at this stage is invaluable as the various foods can be scattered upon it and several chicks can perch around its edge; they seem to learn from each other how to pick up their own food. At each feeding all uneaten material should be removed from the cage before any fresh is supplied, and to prevent any stale particles remaining, which may have been dropped upon the floor, the sand trays should be emptied at least once daily. At this stage it is very useful to have these trays covered with sheets of newspaper instead of sawdust: sawdust is liable to be blown into the food and so be a possible source of trouble to the young birds' digestive systems.

At weaning time it is usual for the breeder to place identification rings upon the legs of his birds, for only in this way can accurate breeding records be kept. These rings are made of lightweight coloured plastic, numbered consecutively, and being 'split' can easily be opened by a special expanding tool and then slipped over the shank of the bird's leg. Such rings are used by British fanciers but on the Continent (and in the case of the Roller canary in

spinach   cabbage

Britain) it is essential to use 'closed' rings which have to be put on when the chicks are still in the nest at about five or six days.

After safely raising the first nest of chicks most canary pairs will successfully rear a second, and even a third, brood. Sometimes, in fact, the hen will be eager to nest again before the first brood is off her hands and this is particularly so when the cock bird has been left with her to help with the rearing. If this appears to be the case a new nest pan must be provided, together with an adequate supply of fresh nesting material, otherwise in obeying her instinct to build again the hen may resort to plucking feathers from the young ones.

Once they are safely weaned and feeding themselves, young canaries should continue to develop and by the age of eight weeks they are almost equal in size to the adults. But they are still babies and must be treated accordingly. Any sudden changes of food should be avoided and hard seed must not be fed too soon, as their young digestive systems are incapable of dealing with it. Soaked seed, soft food, seeding weeds, and grasses, and a little fresh lettuce occasionally, should continue as before and hard seed should not be introduced until the young birds are six weeks old. Even then it should only consist of a few grains scattered over the other food in the feeding tray. The quantity of hard seed can then be gradually increased during the next fortnight until at eight weeks the youngsters can have a normal seed hopper hung on the cage front for a few hours daily, this time period slowly increasing until eventually it can be left on continuously as with adult stock. Even at this stage the supply of other foods should still be provided and continue right up to the beginning of, and even during, the moult.

Moulting

Moulting is an annual process which follows closely upon the breeding season. Occupying a period from about the middle of July to the end of October, it provides the bird with a complete set of new feathers for the ensuing twelve months. It is a somewhat trying time for the fancier, providing him with a fair amount of mess to deal with in the birdroom, and he has to exercise his patience until he can really assess his breeding season's efforts by seeing his young birds in the full maturity of their first adult plumage.

Old hands have a saying that this is the time when birds are made or marred for the show bench, so every effort should be made to procure a quick and healthy moult. To this end it is always advisable to finish with the breeding season's activities in good time. Although individual birds usually take only about six to eight weeks to complete their change of feathers, any late-hatched youngsters may not start to moult until September, which would make them very late in finishing — too late for many of the shows. Moreover, late moulting can have a further effect in the following season when such retarded birds may prove to be unsatisfactory breeders. An early moult during the warm days of summer and early autumn is the ideal which most fanciers strive for.

Once a bird has started to moult it is advisable not to move it until the process is complete and it is therefore an advantage to have all the stock suitably caged as soon as possible after breeding has finished. It is usual to cage potential show birds singly in order to minimize any possible damage to the new plumage which squabbling and feather plucking would certainly cause if it happened to occur among a group. Other birds, including adult breeding stock, can be placed in small groups of two, three, or four in double breeding cages, but, if space permits, even these can with advantage be caged singly to allow for individual attention.

In the past fanciers took a great deal of trouble over the moulting of their birds, often providing them with special draughtproof cages and shading them from sunlight by means of shutters or curtains draped over the cages. The exclusion of draughts is a sensible precaution at all times, and direct sunshine may fade the new plumage which would be a disaster for potential show specimens. Precautions should be taken but the birds should not be unduly coddled in any way: plenty of fresh air and adequate

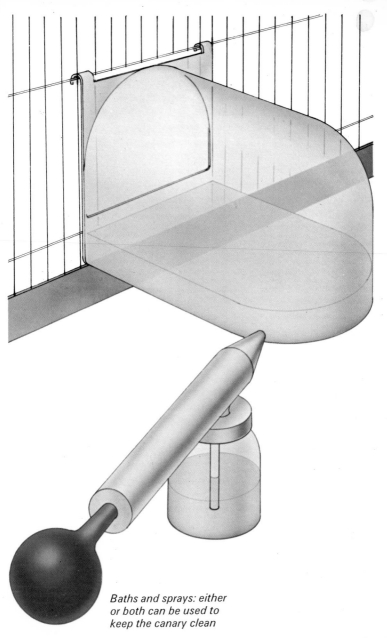

Baths and sprays: either or both can be used to keep the canary clean

exercise are essential for a healthy and vigorous stock.

Baths should be freely provided, except in cold and damp weather; regular bathing, followed by the inevitable preening, has a beneficial effect on the new plumage. Many fanciers actually make a point of lightly spraying their birds during this period, using a small hand syringe for the purpose, but this should not be done late in the day because of the possibility of the birds going to roost with wet plumage.

Although birds should not be moved once they have started to moult, there is no need to suspend the ordinary routine cleaning jobs in cages and birdroom, which need to be carried out at this season just as conscientiously as at any other time. Young birds kept in overcrowded conditions can begin feather plucking and, if not detected, this may result in several birds becoming decidedly bare about the back and rump. Some pieces of partly unravelled string tied to the cage fronts may distract their attention and stop the trouble, but it is always preferable to find the culprits and cage them off separately.

Although moulting is a perfectly natural process it does impose some strain upon the bird's system, for not only has the normal bodily metabolism to be maintained, but material for the new feather structure also has to be provided. This feather tissue is almost entirely formed from proteins so that an adequate supply must be provided in the diet during this period. Many a bird has moulted quite successfully on a good, standard, well-balanced seed mixture but most fanciers provide some extra protein in the form of egg food, two or three times a week, especially in the case of the larger breeds where the young birds continue to grow to some extent during the moult.

At this time of year there is a plentiful supply of wild seeds in the countryside and keen fanciers will go to the trouble of collecting thistle, plantain, dock, shepherd's purse, sowthistle, and so on. In addition to these wild seeds, the regular greenfood supply should be continued both for its vitamin and mineral value and for the improvement it can bring about in colour, especially when using dark-green leaves such as kale or spinach.

The fact that the colour of new feathers could be influenced by the food eaten during the moult was appreciated by fanciers more than a century ago and led to the deliberate practice of 'colour feeding' certain varieties of canary. Originally confined to the Norwich section of the fancy, it was later adopted by Lizard and Yorkshire breeders and, more recently, has been applied to birds

The colour of new feathers can be influenced by the food eaten during the moult

of the Red Factor series. In the case of the three older breeds, the intention is to convert a basically yellow bird into an orange one, and in the Red Factor to turn an already orange bird into a much deeper orange or near-red.

The colouring agents employed for this purpose are incorporated into the birds' softfood which is then fed to them in small quantities daily throughout the duration of the moult. These colour-feeding materials are based on the red-fruited sweet pepper, *Capsicum frutescens grossum,* and on the carotenoid pigment, *Canthaxanthin,* and preparations of them, together with directions for their administration, are obtainable from most fanciers' seedmen and food suppliers. It must be appreciated that the colour change of the plumage is not of a permanent nature so that colour feeding has to be repeated at each successive moult.

As the moulting proceeds it is interesting to follow the sequence of development of the new plumage, which, of course, is particularly easy to see when a young, natural-coloured bird is being colour-fed for the first time. The new feathers can first be seen on the wing butts and then in a narrow band on each side of the breast. This area gradually widens until the entire breast is covered and at the same time new feathers will appear on the back. They also gradually develop and widen and the final replacement of feathers takes place on the head and neck. In its first moult a current-year bird does not replace the flight feathers of its wings and tail, which therefore remain much paler than the rest of the body.

At the conclusion of the moult it still takes a week or so for the plumage to tighten up and to become sleek and glossy; some fanciers will administer chemical tonics in the drinking water at this stage to assist in the hardening-off process and to enable the bird to regain its vigorous health after the rather trying few weeks it has recently undergone. For the next few months the birds are looking just about at their best and it is perhaps not unnatural that this is when the major show season takes place.

Exhibiting

To many fanciers the mere possession and breeding of their canaries is the main source of pleasure, but for the majority their ultimate aim is the show bench. It is only here, by comparing their birds side by side with those of other fanciers, that they can ensure that their breeding efforts are giving the desired results. At the shows they are impartially judged by experienced individuals, with the breed standard as the criterion, so that an unbiased opinion on their merits can be relied upon.

Quite apart from the interest and enjoyment to be obtained from the actual competition, the shows provide so much more, for it is here that fanciers congregate and exchange opinions and experiences, and a great deal can be learned by the newcomer who is prepared to keep his eyes and ears open. Shows are the 'shop windows' of the fancy, and they usually provide the only occasion when members of the general public can see anything of the hobby : they are useful recruiting centres for new hobbyists.

Cage-bird shows range from small, local, members' events, through medium shows, to large-scale 'open' shows, to the great National Exhibition held each December in London, England, where as many as 5,000 canaries may be seen. The new fancier will, in all probability, progress through all of these stages of competition in the course of a few years according to his keenness and ambition. He will start life in the 'Novice' category and, when he has gained the requisite number of wins at this level of competition, will graduate to 'Champion' status.

In many branches of livestock exhibiting, the show authorities provide the necessary exhibition pens on the site for the use of competitors, but this is not so in the case of the canary fancy. Here birds are sent out to the shows in the cages that they will occupy. These 'show cages' are of distinctive patterns designed by the various specialist societies to show off the points of their particular breeds to best advantage, and are the only ones permitted on the show bench. They are readily available from most fanciers' suppliers but it is quite acceptable for anyone to make his own provided that they comply precisely with the approved specifications.

It is of little use merely to put a bird into its show cage and then send it off to a show, for this would result in a bewildered and frightened bird fluttering about the cage as soon as it was touched, or even looked at. A course of training is necessary in order first to accustom the bird to being in a strange cage and then to encourage it to display itself to full advantage when in front of the judge.

The first of these objectives can be tackled at quite an early stage when newly-weaned chicks are about four to five weeks old. If a show cage is hung onto the front of their stock cage, with both doors open to allow them free access, the young birds, being of an inquisitive nature, will soon investigate and enter of their own accord. After a week or so of allowing the birds to familiarize themselves with the situation, they can readily be taught to enter the cage on command by gently guiding them in with a thin piece of wood known as a training stick.

This kind of training can be maintained until the onset of the moult, but the more serious business is generally postponed until its conclusion. Now the show cage with a bird inside can be gently removed and the bird encouraged to adopt the ideal position representative of its breed by scratching the bottom of the cage, lightly touching the wires with the training stick, or using the hand to engage the bird's attention. This requires some degree of patience and should occupy only a minute or so at a time. The trainee should never be allowed to become over-stressed or panicky at this stage, but allowed ample time between sessions to settle down.

What is required of the bird is that it should hold itself up in an alert and intelligent manner as though sharply aware of 'showing off' whenever it is in front of the judge. It should maintain its stance upon the perch and never climb upon the wires or persist in diving onto the floor of the cage. This may sound a tall order in as volatile a bird as a canary, but it is surprising how quickly they learn what is expected of them.

Apart from the training of their birds some fanciers go to even further lengths in preparing them for exhibition, and will hand-wash them a few days prior to a show so that their plumage is in immaculate condition. This is a task perhaps not to be undertaken by a beginner without the advantage of a demonstration of what to do, and preferably the practical assistance of an 'old hand'. In any case, if his birds are kept in perfectly clean conditions and allowed to bathe regularly, hand-washing may not be necessary.

During the course of the season many hundreds of shows are held, usually at the weekend, and the major open events are well advertised in advance in the 'fancy' press. If wishing to enter his birds in one of these, the fancier will have to send away for a

The showcage can be
fixed to the standard cage
so that the canaries can
familiarize themselves
with it

schedule from the show secretary, but, in the case of his local members' show, these are generally sent out as a matter of course to all members concerned. Classification is divided into the previously mentioned 'Novice' and 'Champion' categories, and then, in each of the major breeds, many classes are provided for cocks and hens, yellows and buffs, flighted and unflighted, clear and variegated, and so on. The newcomer to the exhibitors' world must be quite sure of the meaning of all these technical terms when filling in his entry form, or should seek the help of an experienced fancier.

A few days before the show, labels for the cages and travelling cases will be received from the secretary. The stick-on cage labels are fixed on the front of the cage at the lower left hand side, and the travelling case labels are used when the birds are to be sent by public transport. The correct floor covering must be employed in the show cages and this may vary from plain seed for the Norwich and the Yorkshire, oat husks for Borders, to white blotting paper for Lizards — each specialist society having its own ideas of what is best. It is never permissible to use sand or sawdust in show cages because of the mess they would create.

At the shows the birds are in the care of the stewards of the organizing society, who are also responsible for collecting and dispatching them by rail at the beginning and end of the show, the freight charges having been prepaid by the exhibitor. It is also in order for the fancier to deliver and collect his own birds if he so wishes.

In Britain judging is traditionally carried out by means of visual comparison of the exhibits, which are placed in order of merit and seven awards made, namely — First, Second, Third, Fourth, Very Highly Commended, Highly Commended, and Commended. Apart from the class winners, there are also various special prizes to be competed for, such as Best Unflighted, Best Adult, Best Novice, Best Champion, and so on. Monetary prizes are generally very small and even the exhibitor who manages to win several of the 'specials' will barely cover his expenses, especially if he has had to send his birds by rail.

On the Continent, by contrast, a system of points-judging operates in which each exhibit is marked against the official scale of points as laid down by the specialist society, which allocates a specific number of marks to each important feature of the breed. Thus, in any given class, there may well be more than one first prizewinner or, alternatively, no first prizewinner at all if none of

Standard showcage

the exhibits comes up to scratch.

When judging is taking place only show officials are permitted to be present, but when the show is later open to the general public the fancier will naturally be eager to seek out his own exhibits to find out how they have fared. He must learn to take the rough with the smooth, for it is remarkable how one can win one week and lose the next, everything of course depending upon how a bird is actually looking during the crucial few minutes it is before the judge.

Health

For those who keep domestic pets of any description it is generally a matter of pride that their charges are always in vigorous healthy condition and any departure from this can often become a source of worry. The canary fancier is no exception, but it is fortunate that, if kept under conditions of good management, with careful attention to hygiene, adult canaries rarely give much trouble. Birds kept in confinement, of course, no less than those in the wild, can be affected both by diseases and by parasites, and the wise fancier will direct his efforts to prevention rather than to cure.

Correct feeding is an important detail in the avoidance of possible trouble, and the fancier must ensure that all items given are not only of a suitable nature, but also perfectly fresh and free from any kind of contamination. Seeds purchased from a reputable source can always be relied upon but they must be stored carefully in conditions where they are not liable to become musty or fouled by mice or other rodents. Any wild seeds and greenfood offered must also have come from situations where pollution by animals or agricultural sprays is impossible.

After taking precautions as to suitability and freshness of food, it is a sensible follow-up to ensure that any unused food is taken out before it becomes stale. Egg food, greenstuff, and soaked seed should be removed later in the day as they can quickly deteriorate, especially in warm and humid weather conditions.

In spite of all the precautions taken it is still possible that a bird may become ill; it is of course important to identify the symptoms and apply the necessary remedy in good time. It will be readily appreciated that any illness treated in its early stages is much more likely to be eliminated than one of long standing. Pathological examination has identified a great many diseases in birds, almost an alarming number if one reads a specialist work on the subject, but for practical purposes they fall mainly into two groups, in each of which a primary method of treatment can be applied.

The first group of diseases consists of those affecting the respiratory system. These range from mild disorders like hoarseness and a temporary loss of voice due to a cold, to much more serious complaints like asthma, bronchitis, and pneumonia. The chief symptoms in these cases are difficult and laboured breathing, often accompanied by wheezing, rasping, and sneezing. If not eradicated fairly quickly the trouble may become chronic and in the case of pneumonia, death will probably occur in a few days.

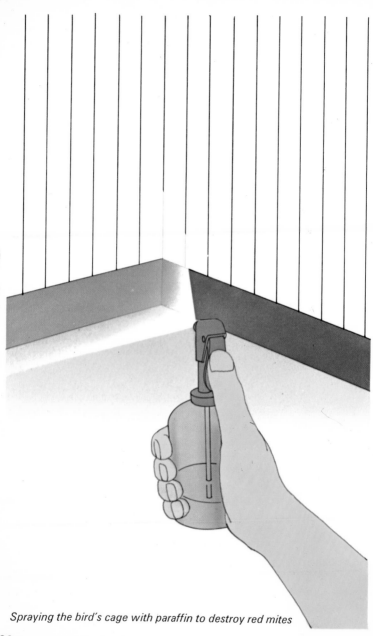

Spraying the bird's cage with paraffin to destroy red mites

Any bird suffering from these symptoms must immediately be isolated to prevent the spread of germs by droplet infection. Old-fashioned fanciers' manuals usually recommend the use of various 'remedies', such as bread and milk, with a few drops of cod-liver oil and a spot or two of whisky added, glycerine, honey and lemon juice in the drinking water, and so on, and in mild cases these may at least act as a palliative until the bird recovers of its own accord. Specially prepared medicines for birds are marketed by several firms of veterinary chemists and are obtainable through pet shops and fanciers' suppliers, and possibly the best course is to purchase one of these and follow the manufacturer's directions. Nearly all of these respiratory complaints are aggravated, or even induced, by bad atmospheric conditions : hence the importance of dry, well-ventilated, draughtproof quarters.

The second class of diseases are those affecting the alimentary system. Septic fever is the one most feared by bird keepers because of its contagious nature. Less serious may be various mild digestive disorders. The causes of these troubles are largely unknown but almost certainly they are initiated by eating stale food or harmful chemicals upon greenstuff or even the paint off the cages. Poor hygiene in the birdroom is another potent source of trouble.

Affected birds become dull and listless, with their feathers fluffed out and their eyes losing their brightness. They usually sleep at intervals during the daytime and wake periodically to pay brief visits to the seed, grit, and water vessels. Trouble may be averted by the early administration of a mild aperient, such as Glauber salts or syrup of buckthorn, to ensure that any offending material has been removed from the system. As in the case of respiratory diseases proprietary medicines prepared by veterinary chemists may be used, but if bacterial infection of the intestinal tract has already occurred, the only real measure is the use of antibiotic drugs, which will need to be prescribed by a veterinary surgeon.

All kinds of livestock are known to be infested at one time or another with various species of external parasites, but the canary fancier is fortunate in that his birds are normally only liable to be affected by two. Under conditions of careful management and good cage sanitation even these can readily be eliminated, and the dedicated fancier usually makes it a point of pride that his stock is free from them. Of these two common species, grey lice are permanent parasites which spend their entire lifespan upon the body of the bird, whereas red mite are intermittent parasites which only come out at night to prey upon their hosts and retire during the daytime into the shelter of cracks and crevices in the wood-work of cages and birdrooms.

The red mite is a blood-sucking creature and if it is present in large numbers is a serious menace to the health of the birds. The prevalence of this pest is most likely to increase during the warm summer months when the mite has a very rapid rate of reproduction. It is not difficult to destroy with one of the anti-mite preparations on the market, but it is important to ensure that the material penetrates deep into their hiding places. Many fanciers follow a routine measure of treating all the likely cracks and joints of the cages with paraffin or turpentine — of course removing the birds until the material has been absorbed by the woodwork and the vapour has dispersed.

Grey lice are not blood-sucking parasites but feed mainly upon skin and feather tissue, causing considerable irritation to the birds. It will be appreciated that only by actually treating the birds them-selves can any attack be made upon this particular pest, and since the lice live deep down among the underflue of feathers, close to the skin, there is always some difficulty in reaching them. The substance to be used is an insecticidal powder, specially marketed for use on pet birds, and it must be dusted liberally into the base of the feathers, especially round the neck, the thighs, and under the wings, at the same time taking care not to allow it to get into the bird's eyes. As the material is not effective against the eggs of the lice, a second and possibly a third application may be necessary at intervals of about ten days.

Should an infestation of lice be detected while the birds are actually breeding, of course it becomes impossible to handle them without the risk of upsetting the whole operation; the fancier will have to decide whether to allow the birds to continue, and deal with the pest at a later date, or to eradicate the parasites first and then allow the birds to go to nest again. Unless the attack is a particularly bad one, most breeders would prefer to take the former course.

If either sickness or parasites have been experienced in the bird-room it is a sensible precaution to clean and disinfect any cages whose occupants have been affected. This can be simply done by thoroughly washing them out with a solution containing any of the well-known household antiseptics at the recommended strength.

Index